NUTRITION
BASICS

by Beth Bence Reinke, MS, RD

Content Consultant
Shahla Ray, PhD
Department of Applied Healthy Science
Indiana University

Core Library

An Imprint of Abdo Publishing
abdopublishing.com

abdopublishing.com

Published by Abdo Publishing, a division of ABDO, PO Box 398166,
Minneapolis, Minnesota 55439. Copyright © 2016 by Abdo Consulting
Group, Inc. International copyrights reserved in all countries. No part of
this book may be reproduced in any form without written permission from
the publisher. Core Library™ is a trademark and logo of Abdo Publishing.

Printed in the United States of America, North Mankato, Minnesota
042015
092015

THIS BOOK CONTAINS
RECYCLED MATERIALS

Cover Photo: Shutterstock Images
Interior Photos: Shutterstock Images, 1, 13, 15, 39; iStockphoto, 4, 6,
10, 18, 21, 24, 45; Lissandra Melo/Shutterstock Images, 30; Alex Skopje/
iStockphoto, 33; Tatyana Vyc/Shutterstock Images, 36

Editor: Mirella Miller
Series Designer: Becky Daum

Library of Congress Control Number: 2015931585

Cataloging-in-Publication Data
Reinke, Beth Bence.
 Nutrition basics / Beth Bence Reinke.
  p. cm. -- (Food matters)
Includes bibliographical references and index.
ISBN 978-1-62403-866-2
1. Nutrition--Juvenile literature.   I. Title.
613.2--dc23
                                                2015931585

CONTENTS

CHAPTER ONE

FOOD, ENERGY, AND YOU

When your stomach rumbles after soccer practice, you need a snack. You used a great deal of energy to run and kick the ball. Now your body feels worn out and hungry. It is time to refuel so you can do homework and play. Which snack will you choose? A banana or a brownie? Chips or a cheese stick? To make smart food choices, you need to know how to identify healthy food.

Eating the right food gives you energy throughout the day.

The body can receive the vitamins it needs through vitamin supplements or food.

Let's Talk about Nutrients

When you eat, your body breaks down food into tiny pieces. Those pieces are called nutrients. Eating food with the right nutrients keeps you healthy. Nutrients help you grow taller, build strong muscles, and have healthy skin. Nutrients from food help build every cell in your body. The old saying is true: You are what you eat!

Food contains six types of nutrients. They are proteins, fats, carbohydrates, vitamins, minerals, and water. Most food contains all six nutrients in different amounts.

Nutrients are divided into two categories. The body needs a large amount of protein, fat, carbohydrates, and water each day. These are macronutrients. *Macro* means big. Vitamins and minerals are micronutrients. *Micro* means small. The body needs only small amounts of vitamins and minerals each day.

YOUR LIFE

Energy In, Energy Out

It is important to have energy balance when exercising. This means the calories taken in by the body equals the calories burned. Use this chart to compare food and exercises worth 100 calories for the average ten-year-old.

Foods Worth 100 Calories	Exercise Needed to Burn 100 Calories
15 almonds	Bike riding for 31 minutes
1 cup (8 oz.) grapes	Swimming for 25 minutes
1/2 cup (4 oz.) vanilla low-fat yogurt	Jogging for 17 minutes
1 cup (8 oz.) oat cereal	Running for 10 minutes
1 cup (8 oz.) unsweetened applesauce	Jumping rope for 17 minutes

Milk 2%

Nutrition Facts

Serving size 8 fl. oz. (245g)
Serving Per Container 8

Calories 130   Calories from Fat 45

Total Fat 5g	8%
Total Carbohydrate 13g	4%
Protein 8g	

Vitamin A 10%	•	Vitamin C 4%
Calcium 30%	•	Iron 0%

Nutrition Facts Label
This chapter discusses calories and nutrients. Check out this nutrition facts label for 2 percent milk. How many calories are in one cup (8 oz.) of milk? Can you find the nutrients on this label? Which of the six nutrients is not listed? How do you know milk contains that nutrient?

Food Gives You Energy

Protein, fat, and carbohydrates provide energy to the body. People need energy for everything they do, such as playing, laughing, and reading. Energy helps move muscles and keeps the heart pumping. Energy is measured in units called calories. Food has different numbers of calories. Children ages 8 to 11 need between 1,400 and 2,200 calories each day.

Active children need extra calories to fuel their bodies. Playing soccer uses more calories than playing video games. And dancing burns more calories than watching television. The more a body moves, the more energy it uses.

Even at rest, the body needs energy to stay alive. Calories keep the body running 24 hours a day. When hunger strikes, it is time to fuel up with healthy food.

Ready, Set, Digest

The average child eats more than 1,000 meals each year. All of the food in these meals is broken down into nutrients. Teeth mash food into pieces and mix it with saliva to make a mushy glob. The glob slides down the esophagus into the stomach. Then the stomach squirts out digestive juices and churns the food into a thick liquid called chyme. The chyme moves into the small intestine where more digestive juices break nutrients into tiny pieces. The nutrients travel through the walls of the small intestine. The body then uses the nutrients for all types of jobs.

CHAPTER TWO

NUTRIENTS THAT GIVE ENERGY

Energy comes from fats, proteins, and carbohydrates. Most food contains a combination of these nutrients. Think about a turkey-and-cheese sandwich. The bread is made mostly of carbohydrates. But it contains some proteins and fats too. The turkey has protein, and the cheese has protein and fats.

A single sandwich can contain a wide variety of different nutrients.

Fat, protein, and carbohydrates contain calories. One gram of protein or carbohydrates has four calories. But each gram of fat has more than twice as many calories as protein and carbohydrates. High-fat foods have many calories.

Good Fats and Bad Fats

Not all fats are bad. Aside from providing energy, fats have special jobs within the body. Fats help cell membranes stay strong. They also help keep the brain, eyes, and nerves working properly. Body fat helps cushion organs to keep them safe. It also helps the body stay warm.

There are different kinds of fats in food. The healthiest fats are oils called unsaturated fats. They are found in seafood and plants. These fats are also found in fish, nuts, seeds, avocados, and olive oil.

The solid fats in meat and dairy are called saturated fats. They can be unhealthy. Man-made fats, called trans fats, are also unhealthy. They are made by

Nuts are just one of the foods that contain unsaturated fats.

changing liquid oils into solid fats. Trans fats are found in margarine, crackers, and some fried food.

Powerful Protein

There is a great deal of protein in some types of food, such as meat, fish, and eggs. Nuts, legumes, and dairy products also have protein. Most of the time, protein is used to build body tissues. If the body does not have enough fats or carbohydrates, it will use protein for energy.

Protein is digested into small pieces called amino acids. Amino acids are similar to tiny building blocks. They fit together in different patterns to make body parts. They build muscles and organs. Protein also makes skin, hair, and blood cells.

Check Out Carbohydrates

Carbohydrates are main sources of energy for the body, especially the brain. Carbohydrates are found mainly in food that comes from plants. Grains, fruits, and vegetables have carbohydrates. But some dairy products, such as milk and yogurt, also contain carbohydrates.

There are two types of carbohydrates

Let's Build Protein

Amino acids are similar to building blocks. Different combinations of amino acids do different things for the body. The body combines amino acids to create different types of protein. One protein might be used in brain cells and another to build muscle. The body uses the 20 different amino acids to make different types of protein.

Grain products, such as bread, contain a lot of carbohydrates.

that provide energy: simple and complex. Simple carbohydrates are also called sugars. Sweet food, such as fruits and cookies, contain sugar. Sugar is small, so the body absorbs it quickly for energy. Complex carbohydrates are also known as starches.

Fad Diets

Have you ever been sick with the stomach flu? You might eat only chicken broth and popsicles for one or two days. That is okay. It gives your digestive system a rest. But sometimes people follow eating plans called fad diets. These people might stop eating carbohydrates for a long time. Or they may eat hardly any fats. Nutrients are missing from fad diets. Your body needs all of the nutrients to be healthy. Have you heard of any fad diets? What kinds of foods could you eat on this diet? After reading this chapter, does this fad diet have all the nutrients your body needs?

Foods such as pasta, bread, and rice contain starches. Starches have many sugars connected together. During digestion, the body takes time to break the starches apart into sugars. This is why complex carbohydrates seem to give the body more energy.

This excerpt is from a college nutrition book. It discusses the six kinds of nutrients found in food:

> . . . a healthy human body is 60 percent water. The other 40 percent is made up of protein and fat, as well as a small amount of stored carbohydrates, minerals in the bone, and small amounts of vitamins. Thus, the old saying is true: we are what we eat, from the carbohydrates in broccoli to the proteins in meat; the six biochemical ingredients needed to sustain life are all provided by the foods in our diets.

Source: Joan Salge Blake, Kathy D. Munoz, and Stella Volpe. Nutrition: From Science to You. Glenview, IL: Pearson Education, Inc., 2014. Print. 8.

What's the Big Idea?

Read this passage carefully. What is the authors' main point about food, nutrients, and the body? Find two details they use to make this point. What can you tell about nutrients and the body from these details?

NUTRIENTS WITH SPECIAL JOBS

More than 100 years ago, scientists believed tiny nutrients in food helped keep people alive. They were right! Some of these micronutrients are minerals, which come from the earth. The other nutrients are substances called vitamins. *Vita* means life.

Vitamins and minerals in food may be tiny, but they are mighty. They aid in almost every process that

Eating a variety of colorful fruits and vegetables provides the body with the vitamins and minerals it needs.

keeps the body healthy. If one vitamin or mineral is missing from the body, you will become sick.

Two Kinds of Vitamins

There are two kinds of vitamins—fat soluble and water soluble. The fat-soluble vitamins are A, D, E, and K. Vitamin A is found in egg yolks, carrots, and apricots. Fish contain vitamin D. For vitamin E, munch on almonds or sunflower seeds. Vitamin K is found in leafy greens, such as raw kale and turnip greens. These four vitamins need fats from food to be absorbed. The body stores fat-soluble vitamins in the liver and body fat until it needs to use them. For example, the body might use some of its stored vitamin D to help build bones.

Water-soluble vitamins move through the body with water. Vitamin C and all of the B vitamins are water soluble. There are eight different B vitamins. They are found in many types of food, such as whole grains, eggs, meats, leafy vegetables, and dried beans. Most of the B vitamins help the body

Citrus fruits, such as oranges, grapefruit, lemons, and limes, contain vitamin C.

get energy from food. Strawberries, cantaloupe, tomatoes, and bell peppers contain vitamin C.

It is essential to eat food with water-soluble vitamins every day. The body does not keep these vitamins to be used later. Any extra B vitamins or vitamin C leaves the body each day through urine.

Many Minerals

Minerals come from soil and water. As spinach grows, it gets iron and calcium from the dirt. When people

YOUR LIFE

Be a Vitamin and Mineral Detective

Some types of food have vitamins or minerals added to them. Milk is fortified with vitamin D because it is hard to get enough of this vitamin in a daily diet. Vitamin D is important because it works with calcium to build strong bones and teeth. Bread and pasta are enriched with B vitamins. These vitamins are reduced when flour is refined. Many cereals have vitamins and minerals added too. Read the label on a multivitamin bottle. Can you find all of the names of the vitamins? The B vitamins have both a letter name and a word name. Now look at the ingredients lists on milk, bread, and your favorite cereal. How many vitamins and minerals can you find?

eat spinach, they receive these nutrients too. Animals that eat plants get minerals the same way, which they pass on to humans who eat animal products. When cows eat grass, the minerals enter their milk and meat. When people drink cow's milk, they receive calcium. People receive iron from eating cow meat.

Calcium's special job is helping bones grow strong. Iron keeps the whole body alive. It carries oxygen from the lungs to each cell in the body.

Sodium and potassium work hand-in-hand to keep body fluids in balance.

What about Water?

The most important fluid is water. More than half of a body's weight is from water. That is why a body needs more water than any other nutrient. Water is essential for every job in the body. People cannot store water, so drinking enough of it each day is a must.

FURTHER EVIDENCE

Chapter Three focuses on vitamins and minerals. What was one of the chapter's main points? What pieces of evidence in the chapter support this main point? Check out the website at the link below. Does the information on this website support the main point in this chapter? Write a few sentences using new information from the website as evidence to support the main point in this chapter.

Eat a Rainbow
mycorelibrary.com/nutrition-basics

CHAPTER FOUR

FOOD TO EAT EVERY DAY

F ood stops a rumbling stomach, but some food is better than others. The healthiest food is nutrient dense. A nutrient-dense food has protein, carbohydrates, or healthy fats. It also may have vitamins, minerals, and fiber.

Nutrient-dense food nourishes the body better than junk food. That is why the US Department of Agriculture (USDA) recommends nutritious food to

Blueberries are a nutrient-dense food, full of vitamin K and fiber.

eat every day. In 1980 the USDA released the first edition of *Dietary Guidelines for Americans*. These helpful tips show people how to eat healthfully. Nutrition experts update the nutrition goals every five years.

The MyPlate Guide

More than 20 years ago, the USDA created a pyramid graphic to go along with the dietary goals. The pyramid shows people how much of each kind of food to eat every day. In 2011 a colorful new graphic called MyPlate was released. It shows a plate and a cup divided

What Does a Serving Look Like?

Sometimes you may want to measure food with a scale or measuring cups. Other times it is easier to estimate how much food is on your plate. You can use these tips to get a sense of common serving sizes.

- ½ cup (4 oz.) rice or pasta = a tennis ball
- 1 cup (8 oz.) fruit or veggies = a baseball
- 2 tablespoons peanut butter = a ping-pong ball
- 1.5 ounces (43 g) cheese = a 9-volt battery
- ¼ cup (2 oz.) dried fruit = an egg
- 3 ounces (85 g) meat = a deck of cards or a cell phone

into five food groups: fruits, vegetables, protein, grains, and dairy.

There is no place on the MyPlate graphic for fats. That is because fats are inside many other foods, such as meat, fish, and nuts. Fats and oils are part of a healthy diet. Children ages 9 to 13 need approximately 5 teaspoons (25 g) of fats and oils each day.

MyPlate on Your Plate

It is easy to use MyPlate as a guide at mealtime. Choose different-colored fruits and vegetables to fill half the plate. Put protein and grains on the other half of the plate. Top off the meal with a glass of milk.

Loading half of the plate with colorful fruits and vegetables is good for health because they are nutrient-dense food. Whole fruits have more fiber than juice. Fiber helps us feel full and pushes food through the digestive tract. Whole grains are high in fiber too. They are made with every part of a grain seed. When grains are processed, the nutritious parts

Food Group	Amount Needed Each Day	What Equals 1 Cup
Fruit	1.5 cups (12 oz.)	1 cup (8 oz.) fruit 1 cup (8 oz.) 100 percent fruit juice 0.5 cup (4 oz.) dried fruit
Vegetables	1.5 to 2.5 cups (12 to 20 oz.)	1 cup (8 oz.) raw or cooked vegetables 1 cup (8 oz.) vegetable juice 2 cups (16 oz.) raw, leafy greens 1 medium baked potato
Dairy	2.5 to 3 cups (20 to 24 oz.)	1 cup (8 oz.) milk 1 cup (8 oz.) yogurt 1.5 ounces (43 g) cheese

Food Group	Amount Needed Each Day	What Equals 1 Ounce or Ounce Equivalent
Protein	4 to 5 ounces (113 to 142 g)	1 ounce (28 g) meat, poultry, or fish 1 egg 1 tablespoon (15 g) peanut butter 0.5 ounce (14 g) nuts or seeds 0.25 cup (40 g) cooked legumes
Grains	5 to 6 ounces (142 to 170 g)	1 slice bread 1 cup (8 oz.) dry cereal 0.5 cup (4 oz.) cooked oatmeal 0.5 cup (4 oz.) rice or pasta 1 small tortilla

Eating Your Food Groups

Do you eat veggies for breakfast? If not, that is okay. You can eat them for lunch and dinner instead. Children need 2 to 2.5 cups (16 to 20 oz.) of fruits and vegetables each day. Use this chart to figure out how much children age 8 to 11 should be eating each day.

of a grain seed are removed. That is why refined grains have less fiber, vitamins, and minerals. White bread and white rice are refined grains. Eating whole grains adds more fiber to a diet.

Chicken, fish, and lean beef contain healthy protein. Other types of food, such as eggs, legumes, beans, and nuts, are good choices for protein too. Whole milk has more fat than low-fat milk, but both are nutrient-dense drinks. You can use these tips to fill up your MyPlate at each meal.

YOUR LIFE
Find the Fiber

Choosing to eat whole grains is one way to get fiber. Another way is to eat plenty of fruits and vegetables. Whole fruits are more nutritious than fruit juice. Fiber and most of the vitamins and minerals are found in the flesh and skin of fruits. A small apple with skin has 3.5 grams of fiber, while an apple without the skin has only 1.5 grams of fiber. A ½-cup serving of applesauce also has 1.5 grams of fiber. Even 1 cup of apple juice contains 0.5 grams of fiber. Which has more fiber? Which would you choose to eat more often?

CHAPTER FIVE

FOOD TO EAT SOMETIMES

There is a nickname for food that contains a large amount of sugar, fat, or salt. It is junk food. French fries, candy bars, and doughnuts are examples of junk food. They are called "junk" because they have many calories but few vitamins or minerals. Eating junk food every day is not healthy, but eating it once in a while is okay.

Many vending machines are full of foods that are not healthy.

Added Sugar

Sweet drinks get most of their calories from added sugar. Sugar is empty calories. Limiting added sugars to no more than 6 teaspoons (30 g) per day is best.

8 oz. (30 g) drink	Grams of sugar	Teaspoons of sugar
fruit punch	28	5.7
cola	26	5.3
juice drink	25	5.1
sweet tea	22	4.5
ginger ale	21	4.3
sports drink	13	2.6
water	0	0

Empty Calories

Fruits and dairy products contain natural sugar and are nutritious. They have vitamins and minerals the body needs. But food that contains added sugar is not healthy. Added sugar refers to the extra sugar put into food during cooking. Children in the United States get approximately 23 teaspoons (113 g) of added sugar per day. Much of it comes from sweet drinks and desserts. Soda, sweet tea, cookies, and cakes are full of empty calories.

It is best to avoid trans fat in foods, if possible.

Solid fats are full of empty calories too. There are two kinds of solid fats—saturated fats and trans fats. Saturated fats are found in many types of food, including meat and cheese. Sausage, hot dogs, and bacon have a great deal of saturated fat. People should eat these types of food only sometimes.

Trans fats are the worst fats. They are harmful to the body. Trans fats are found mostly in junk food, such as bakery goods, fried food, and snack food. Margarine and ready-to-use frosting are examples. Eating no trans fats at all on most days is the healthiest plan.

YOUR LIFE
Do Not Supersize Me

What would you order at a fast-food restaurant? Even small servings of fast food have too much salt and fat. It is okay to eat fast food once in a while, but you do not have to eat greasy, salty, sugary food at every meal. You can make healthier choices.

Instead of:	Choose:
cheeseburger with bacon	hamburger with tomato and lettuce
large fries	fruits or small fries
chicken nuggets	grilled chicken sandwich
onion rings	side salad
milkshake	low-fat chocolate milk
soda	100 percent fruit juice or bottled water

Sodium is found in salty foods. Sodium is a mineral the body needs, but too much sodium is not healthy. Lunch meats, hot dogs, and fast food contain a large amount of sodium.

Cutting Back

There are easy ways to eat less added sugar, fat, and sodium. You can eat smaller amounts of food that contain these empty calories. Junk food is not the best fuel for the body and should only be eaten as a special treat.

Joy Bauer is a registered dietitian. In her book she discusses sweets:

> So your favorite sugary sweets are classified as carbohydrates—and you're supposed to eat a lot of carbohydrates—so it's okay to load up on gummy bears and licorice, right?
>
> Not a chance. Here's why: . . . Simple sugars such as candy, sodas, and sugary sweeteners found in cakes and cookies offer little in the form of nutrition except providing your body with energy and calories. These foods are literally "empty calories"—calories with no nutritional value.
>
> In moderation, simple sugars are perfectly fine, but people who consistently load up on the sweet stuff often find themselves too full for, or uninterested in, the healthy foods their bodies require.

Source: Joy Bauer. The Complete Idiot's Guide to Total Nutrition. Indianapolis: Pearson Education, Inc., 2003. Print. 17.

Consider Your Audience

Read this passage carefully. Consider how you would adapt it for a different audience, such as your parents or friends. Write a blog post conveying this same information for the new audience. How does your new approach differ from the original text and why?

CHAPTER SIX

HEALTHY CHOICES MATTER

S hould you eat a chicken patty or a tuna sandwich? Ride your bike or play a video game? Drink a soda or a glass of milk? These are the kinds of decisions you make every day. Making good choices helps keep your body healthy. Using MyPlate to make a balanced meal is a good start. Munching on nutrient-dense fruits and vegetables throughout the day also is a good idea. Other healthy

Eating a healthy breakfast is a good way to start the day.

food options include choosing whole-grain cereal with no added refined sugar or picking low-fat milk over a sugary drink.

No one makes perfect food choices all the time. Having a treat sometimes is okay. But making unhealthy choices over and over can lead to health problems. Nutrition experts say too many children are overweight. In the past 30 years, the number of obese children in the United States has quadrupled. Obesity has become a health problem.

Exercise helps strengthen muscles, build strong bones, and maintain a healthy weight.

Get Up and Play

Being a couch potato can help people gain weight. Watching television, using a computer, or playing video games are not active play. The only muscles getting exercise are in the fingers. Sitting does not burn as many calories as running and playing. Children need to exercise for about one hour each day. They can do a whole hour of active play at one time, or they can do short bursts of exercise that add up to 60 minutes for the day.

Growing Up Healthy

Each year the doctor or school nurse checks your growth. Your body mass index (BMI) is calculated using your height and weight. The BMI number estimates total body fat. A higher number may mean a person has more body fat. BMI is a way to check growth. Comparing your height, weight, and BMI from last year shows how much you have grown. You may grow faster or slower than a friend or sibling. That is okay. Every body is unique and special. Height and weight are partly decided by your family genes.

You Can Make Healthy Choices

The body has a built-in system for energy balance. A hungry stomach means it is time to eat. Feeling full is the signal to stop eating. But sometimes it is easy to ignore those feelings. A boy who has to clean his plate to earn dessert might eat past fullness. A girl who sees a television commercial for candy might eat chocolate when she is not truly hungry.

When you learn about nutrition, you know which types of food are healthy. You can tune out bad advice from television ads or friends. You can listen to your body to detect when you are hungry or full. And you can use your brain to make smart decisions about food and exercise. There are many easy and fun ways to take care of your body. You can drink water or eat a piece of fruit. You can move your muscles by playing outdoors. What healthy choices will you make today?

EXPLORE ONLINE

The focus in Chapter Six is making healthy food and exercise choices. It also touches on childhood obesity. The website below focuses on physical activity and ways children can eat healthy. As you know, every source is different. How is the information given in the website different from the information in this chapter? Which information is the same? How do the two sources present information differently? What can you learn from this website?

Let's Move Campaign
mycorelibrary.com/nutrition-basics

- Food provides calories and nutrients needed for proper growth and development.
- Calories fuel all the body's activities when at rest and when exercising.
- Macronutrients—proteins, fats, and carbohydrates—provide energy to fuel the body's activities.
- Micronutrients—vitamins and minerals—do many special jobs that keep the body healthy.
- Eating a variety of healthy foods, including colorful fruits and vegetables, helps children be healthy.
- Using the MyPlate guide helps children learn how to fill their plates with healthy food choices at each meal.
- Replacing food that is high in fat and sugar with nutritious food contributes to good health.
- Exercising for one hour every day helps children grow up strong and healthy.

IN THE KITCHEN

Berry Good Banana Split

1 small banana, peeled

½ cup low-fat vanilla yogurt

1 tablespoon granola

½ cup fresh strawberries and blueberries

Cut the banana in half lengthwise. Then spoon yogurt into a bowl. Place a banana half on each side of the yogurt. Top with granola and berries. Enjoy!

STOP AND THINK

Why Do I Care?

Maybe you don't eat junk food all the time. But that doesn't mean that you don't have an unhealthy snack sometimes. How can eating junk food affect your body and your health? How does choosing healthy food make your life better? Why are vitamins and minerals important? Which of your favorite foods are rich in vitamins and minerals?

Take a Stand

This book talks about making healthy food choices. Imagine you are having breakfast at a friend's house. There are two boxes of cereal on the kitchen table. One is made with whole grains and has raisins and almonds in it. The other is colorful and sugary. Which cereal would you choose to eat? Why would you make this choice?

You Are There

This book discusses using MyPlate to make healthy food choices. Imagine you are going through the cafeteria line. Think about where each food belongs on MyPlate. Which food groups did you fill? Name the foods you placed on your tray. Why are they good choices?

Say What?

Studying nutrition can mean learning a lot of new vocabulary. Find five words in this book you've never heard before. Use a dictionary to find out what they mean. Then write the meanings in your own words and use each word in a new sentence.

GLOSSARY

carbohydrates
various substances found
in foods that are made of
carbon, hydrogen, and oxygen

enriched
having vitamins or minerals
added back in after being
reduced during processing

fortified
having vitamins or minerals
added in that are not
naturally found in a food

macronutrients
nutrients the body requires in
large amounts

micronutrients
nutrients the body requires in
small amounts

protein
a nutrient that provides
energy for the body

refined grains
food that has the most
nutritious parts of the
grain seed removed during
processing

saturated fats
solid fats found mostly in
food, such as meat and dairy,
that comes from animals

trans fats
solid fats created from
vegetable oils

unsaturated fats
oils found mostly in fish,
vegetables, and nuts

whole grains
food made with the whole
grain seed and containing
vitamins, minerals, and fiber

LEARN MORE

Books

Petrie, Kristin. *Food and Energy: Striking a Healthy Balance.* Minneapolis: Abdo Publishing, 2012.

Petrie, Kristin. *Food Buzz: Nutrition in the News.* Minneapolis: Abdo Publishing, 2012.

Rissman, Rebecca. *Eating Organic.* Minneapolis: Abdo Publishing, 2016.

Websites

To learn more about Food Matters, visit **booklinks.abdopublishing.com.** These links are routinely monitored and updated to provide the most current information available.

Visit **mycorelibrary.com** for free additional tools for teachers and students.

INDEX

ABOUT THE AUTHOR

Beth Bence Reinke is a registered dietitian with degrees in biology and nutrition. She uses her background in education and pediatric nutrition to help children learn about healthy eating.